SONGS
BY THIRTY AMERICANS

Da Capo Press Music Reprint Series

MUSIC EDITOR
BEA FRIEDLAND
Ph.D., City University of New York

This title was recommended for Da Capo reprint by
Paul Glass
Professor Emeritus, Brooklyn College

SONGS
BY THIRTY AMERICANS

EDITED BY
RUPERT HUGHES

FOR HIGH VOICE

DA CAPO PRESS · NEW YORK · 1977

Library of Congress Cataloging in Publication Data

Hughes, Rupert, 1872-1956, ed.
    Songs by thirty Americans.

    (Da Capo Press music reprint series)
    Reprint of the 1904 ed. published by O. Ditson,
Boston, which was issued as v. [13] of The Musicians
library.
    1. Songs (High voice) with piano. 2. Songs,
American. I. Title. II. Series: The Musicians
library (Boston); v. 13.
M1619.H88 1977 [M1629] 784'.306 77-1942
ISBN 0-306-70824-8

This Da Capo Press edition of *Songs by Thirty Americans*
is an unabridged republication of the first edition
published in Boston in 1904.

Published by Da Capo Press, Inc.
A Subsidiary of Plenum Publishing Corporation
227 West 17th Street, New York, N. Y. 10011

SONGS
BY THIRTY AMERICANS

SONGS
BY THIRTY AMERICANS

EDITED BY

RUPERT HUGHES

FOR HIGH VOICE

THE
MUSICIANS
LIBRARY

BOSTON : OLIVER DITSON COMPANY

NEW YORK : CHAS. H. DITSON & CO. CHICAGO : LYON & HEALY

PHILADELPHIA : J. E. DITSON & CO.

D. B. UPDIKE, THE MERRYMOUNT PRESS, BOSTON

CONTENTS

CONTENTS

INDEX

SONGS BY THIRTY AMERICANS

IT was only the other day that Tennyson's allusion to

The early pipe of half-awakened birds

would have served famously to describe the state of affairs in the uncleared forest of American music.

It was only the other day that the whole literature of American composition might have deserved that heinous slander Mark Twain so winningly sent forth against the delectable works of Miss Jane Austen, when he said that they were the only volumes the absence of which from any library argued for its completeness. Yesterday it had been no slander to say that American music had a purely algebraic value. When you subtract a minus quantity from anything, you add to it. So the absence of American composers from a musical program was, so far as it went, a proof of discriminating culture.

But that was yesterday. This is to-day.

The deliberate Portuguese say, "Patience! tomorrow is another day!" And American music has large hopes of its *Mañana*. But meanwhile, we have also a to-day that is neither without its comforts, nor empty of pride.

For one thing, the American composer is suffering from something that looks a little like prosperity. It is hardly more than a symptom, but the pleasant disease is at work: it has fastened on the body musical of America. And, in spite of a common public fallacy that genius always dies of starvation, the fact is, of course, that periods of great and lasting artistic glory have practically always been periods of distinct personal success for the artists. Witness the ages of Perikles and Augustus, the Renaissance, the Elizabethan and Victorian eras, when artists got money from patron or publisher, wore good clothes and moved in an atmosphere of elegance. To say then that the American composer is beginning to achieve money and pub-

licity, is almost tantamount to saying that he is deserving of both; for, after all, you cannot have a Golden Age without gold, and, by corollary, an age of gold has an excellent chance of being a Golden Age.

To show how much the estate of the composer has been mollified in this country, I may not be begrudged a little personal reminiscence. Less than ten years ago, I devoted to American composers a long series of magazine articles, later revised in book-form. The material for this work was chiefly found in the unpublished works of the composers. The constant wail was, "To see me at my best, you must study my manuscripts. The publishers won't look at my good works, and neither will the performers." In those days—it seems they must have been ante-bellum days—the public singer, pianist or conductor who included an American name in his program was looked at with amazement as straining after eccentricity. A critic of prominence could say with all blandness: "I never go near a concert of native works;" and echo answered, "I don't blame him."

Then the tide turned. Or, rather, it moved; it had never gone high enough to be a tide or take an ebb before. With tide-like stealth and breadth it came in. To-day the American composer does not need to be isolated like a pest to a ward of his own. His name is seen on almost every program, —mingling with the classics and the European standards in democratic good-fellowship. And no one notes any special lack of mind or heart in the native music. The American march and dance tune have swept the world as no others of the day; and the more elaborate forms of oratorio, cantata, sonata and song are by no means infrequent in London, Berlin, Munich, Paris or Florence. At home the names of a few prominent men of the better class are almost household words, and their works almost household music.

The contrast with the condition ten years ago

is amazing; to me it is almost painful, for where at that time the composer was begging me to look at his unprintable manuscripts, now, to-day, when I am asked to compile this collection, and when I send out a gracious permission to submit manuscripts, the answer comes from almost everywhere: "I regret that all my manuscripts are printed and I am under contract for some years to such and such a publisher to give him all I can write." Yesterday I was greeted as a welcome stranger; to-day as a solicitor, a bore. It has been difficult, therefore, to compile this work, and to make it truly representative, as I think it is, of how excellently well the Yankee can write music when he sets his heart and brain upon it.

The history of American music is a short story. It could be compressed into an epigram—if one could only think of the epigram. Everything that preceded the Civil War could be lost without loss, except enough to fill a toy Noah's ark. Into this you would put a few captivating jigs like *The Arkansas Traveller*; perhaps a hymn or two of Lowell Mason's—if you like hymns; a few of Stephen C. Foster's folk-tunes that cuddle in the heart; that inexpressibly joyous *Dixie*, which the South borrowed from an Ohio minstrel whose negro-ness was only burnt-cork-deep, and which the North has since reclaimed in its war-won sanctity. You would save these tunes and a few of the more genuine and more sterling melodies of the slaves. The rest you could let go without a sigh. *Yankee Doodle* and *The Star-Spangled Banner* could be renewed from their original sources abroad. Even *Columbia the Gem of the Ocean* is either an English tune, or, if written in America, was written by an Englishman by the reminiscent name of Thomas à Becket.

It is hard to realize what parvenus American composers are. The name of Raff has a distinctly modern, a recent sound in European music. Yet his 205th opus and his 8th symphony, *Frühlingsklänge*, was written in 1878, a year before John Knowles Paine's similarly named *Spring* symphony, which was only the second symphony of the most venerable American composer,—the very first worth serious consideration. When our

Civil War broke out, Paine was only twenty-two years old and was still studying in Germany, where all our reputable composers were trained in the early days—if one may use the word "early" of so late a matter.

In 1865 Paine made a concert tour of Germany as an organist; and in 1867 he conducted at Berlin his Mass. His splendid oratorio, *St. Peter*, produced at Portland, Maine, in 1873, was the first and for some time the only real oratorio this country could boast—and this country has always done well at boasting. Paine's first, and therefore America's first, symphony was conducted by Theodore Thomas in 1876, the same year that saw the culmination of German dramatic music in the first performance of Wagner's *Ring of the Nibelungs*, at Bayreuth. Paine, too, has written a grand opera, *Azara*, to his own libretto, but its production is not yet visible to the naked eye on the horizon of the twentieth century. Nor is the production of any other American grand opera worthy of the name to be recorded in the scrolls of the past, or espied in the promises of the future.

But all this is not to say that because American music is new, it is therefore worthless. Rather has it an advantage of its newness, for it begins when music is no longer struggling to make its tools and its technic before it can chisel its thought. Of American music at its best, in all its youthful greenness, you might quote the lines in which Theokritos described the ivy-wood bowl that was offered to the singer Thyrsis for his song. The translation is Marion Miller's and the lines picture the chalice as

Wrought so newly that still the wood hath a savor
That tangs of the tool of the graver.

The point to be remembered, then, in praise of what American music has attained, and in excuse for what it has not yet done, is, that a line drawn through the year 1865 would include on its hither side practically every effort at composition that an American composer has ever made with proper tools and training and serious intent.

It is not the purpose of this book to indicate the genuinely good work done by native art in the fields of the symphony, the overture, the oratorio, the chamber-music, or instrumental music of any sort. This book is solely an anthology of American songs, not claiming completeness, but asking acceptance as a group of lyrics by thirty men who are fairly representative of American achievement. As they are all contemporaries, and almost all alive, and as no two persons would agree on the order of precedence,—if indeed even one person could agree with himself on so foolish a whim,—it will save trouble to arrange in chronological order the brief notices that must serve to introduce them to your consideration.

Rupert Hughes

New York, May, 1904.

BIOGRAPHICAL SKETCHES

JOHN KNOWLES PAINE (1839)

John K. Paine.

The biography of Professor Paine, born in Portland, Maine, January 9, 1839, and his musical importance have been already discussed in the introduction.

The *Matin Song*, which represents him here, is a lyric of simple fervor and distinctly singable melodic outlines.

DUDLEY BUCK (1839)

Dudley Buck

A composer who was born at Hartford, Connecticut, March 10, 1839, only two months later than J. K. Paine, is Mr. Dudley Buck, and he has been perhaps equally influential in overcoming the inertia of the American public toward native music. At the age of nineteen Paine went to Berlin, and the same year Buck went to Leipzig. There he studied composition under Hauptmann and Richter, orchestration under Rietz, and piano under Moscheles and Plaidy. Later he studied the organ with Schneider of Dresden, and after a year more at Paris, returned to Hartford as church organist and teacher. He began a series of organ concert tours lasting fifteen years; they were invaluable to the American public in educating it to the best music. In 1869 Mr. Buck settled in Chicago. In 1871, in the great fire, he lost many manuscripts, and went to Boston to live. He served for some years as assistant conductor to Theodore Thomas, and settled in Brooklyn, where he has since remained.

Though he is chiefly known as a writer of church and organ music, and has attained the foremost place among Americans in these fields, Mr. Buck has also written secular works, large and small, such as his *Centennial Meditations of Columbia*, written on a national commission for the Philadelphia Centennial in 1876, and performed by a choir of one thousand voices and an orchestra of a hundred pieces; a cantata, *The Voyage of Columbus*, which has been given in Germany; a long adaptation from *The Light of Asia*, which was given in London; *The Golden Legend*, which won the Cincinnati prize of one thousand dollars; a symphonic overture, *Marmion*; and other works in which his ambition has not overdrawn his resources. As an example of the distinctly lyric quality and the mellow harmony which characterize all his work, his song *In Thy Dreams* will serve excellently in its tender serenade spirit.

HOMER N. BARTLETT (1845)

Homer N. Bartlett.

A prolific composer is Mr. Bartlett, and he has been writing for many years; but unlike the majority of composers, who began by writing popular music in this country, he has improved constantly and has kept pace with modernity. Some of his early compositions attained a tremendous vogue of a sort that Mr. Bartlett would not now desire. Many of his later works deserve the favor of the most discriminating.

He was born December 28, 1845, at Olive, New York, of old New England stock. He sang correctly before he could speak, at eight was a public violinist, and at fourteen a church organist. His teachers in piano were Mills, Guyon and Pease; in organ composition Jacobson and Braun. He never studied abroad, though some of his teachers were of foreign birth. He has spent most of his life in New York as organist and teacher. For the orchestra he has written an instrumentation of a Chopin Polonaise, and a violin Concertstück. He has partially completed an oratorio, an opera and a cantata. His song *Look not Upon Me with Thine Eyes* shows him in his more serious vein.

ADOLPH M. FOERSTER (1854)

Robert Franz, like Wagner, Browning and many another, confessed with regret that his work was first truly appreciated in America. One of the earliest admirers and disciples of Franz was Mr. Foerster, who for eighteen years carried on an extensive correspondence with him. Mr. Foerster shows in his songs the Franzian preference for the text of the poem to the catchiness of melody. He has written numerously for the orchestra, and some chamber-music, notably two quartets for violin, viola, 'cello and piano.

While his descent is German, and his education also, he was born at Pittsburg, Pennsylvania, February 2, 1854, and has always lived there, excepting three years spent in Leipzig as a student, and a year in Indiana as a teacher. His teachers were Coccius and Wenzel for the piano; Grill and Schimon for singing; for theory E. F. Richter and Papperitz. Aside from a number of piano compositions, including two excellent concert études, the second of which, *Lamentation*, is remarkably full of emotion, Mr. Foerster is chiefly known as a song-writer. His subjects range widely. He has stepped aside from the beaten track in choosing for his lyrics many poems by such older masters as Byron, who is much neglected by song-writers of to-day; and by setting a number of songs which are devoid of what might be called "human interest," in a narrower sense, and are devoted to the moods of nature. Mr. MacDowell has also written such songs. An excellent example of Mr. Foerster's broad manner is his lyric episode *Tristram and Iseult*, a setting of words selected from Matthew Arnold's poem of that title.

WILSON G. SMITH (1855)

A prominent member of the busy colony of musicians at Cleveland, Ohio, is Mr. Smith, who was also born in Ohio, at Elyria, August 19, 1855. He studied at Cincinnati under Otto Singer, then went to Berlin for two years and studied with Kullak, Kiel, Scharwenka, Moszkowski and Oscar Raif. Since 1882 he has lived in Cleveland as teacher, writer, critic and composer. His piano compositions include many very graceful numbers, and several books of technical studies which have taken a high place. In his songs he seeks a simplicity which is often very deep, and full of the highest art. The song represented herewith, *Kiss me, Sweetheart*, is light, but full of lilting ardor.

JAMES H. ROGERS (1857)

A song-writer who in spite of popular success has preferred to write little and polish much is a phenomenon unusual enough to be welcome. Such a man is James H. Rogers, who was born at Fair Haven, Connecticut, February 7, 1857. He began studying the piano at the age of twelve, and at eighteen went to Berlin as a pupil of Loeschhorn, Roeder, Haupt and Erlich, for two years. Thereafter he studied two years in Paris with Guilmant, Fissot and Widor. He then settled in Cleveland,

Ohio, and has since lived there as teacher, organist, concert pianist and publisher. He is an important contribution to the Cleveland colony of musicians, a busy little colony, which includes such composers as Johann H. Beck, Wilson G. Smith and Miss Patty Stair.

Mr. Rogers' lyrics are of many sorts, and remind one of the lyrics of Thomas Bailey Aldrich for their perfect art that does not hamper but enforces the sincerity, and for their passionate compression. His song *April Weather* is an instance of his loyalty to the text in its mad rush of springtime joy.

HENRY BICKFORD PASMORE (1857)

In the San Francisco colony a prominent place has been taken by Mr. H. B. Pasmore, born at Jackson, Wisconsin, June 27, 1857. He went to Germany for his musical education, and studied at the Leipzig Conservatory with Jadassohn, Reinecke and Papperitz. Upon his return to this country he settled on the Pacific coast, and is known as one of the foremost teachers of voice and composition in that section of the country. Though a busy man, he has found time to write many songs and part-songs, besides works for orchestra, a mass and the score of an opera. His *Northern Romance*, included in this collection, is a

striking setting of Andrew Lang's sombre poem, with whose mood the music shows great sympathy, and whose color it dramatically emphasizes.

CLAYTON JOHNS (1857)

One of the most prolific and successful of American songwriters is Clayton Johns. His fertility is largely due, no doubt, to singleness of purpose, for, with the exception of a Berceuse and a Scherzino for the violin, which have been played by the Boston Symphony Orchestra, a chorus for women's voices with string orchestra, a few part-songs and a little music for violin or piano, Mr. Johns has devoted himself strictly to lyric expression.

He was born at New Castle, Delaware, November 24, 1857, of American parents. He first took up architecture as a profession, but gave it up for music. His American teachers were the brilliant critic, William F. Apthorp, John K. Paine, and the eminent native pianist, William H. Sherwood. Mr. Johns then went abroad, and at Berlin studied under Kiel, Grabau, Reif and Franz Rummel. Upon his return to America he took up his residence in Boston, and is a prominent factor in the musical life of that city. His song *If Love were not* is typical of his fluent melody and unstrained effects.

HARRY ROWE SHELLEY (1858)

Mr. Shelley has the distinction of having composed one or two of the most popular songs ever written in this country, and at the same time of succeeding in more serious and larger forms, such as his notable symphony, his very successful oratorio *The Inheritance Divine*, two manuscript operas, a symphonic poem, a dramatic overture, a suite, and much music for the piano and organ.

He was born at New Haven, Connecticut, June 8, 1858, and studied under Gustave J. Stoeckel, who was professor of music at Yale University before Professor Horatio W. Parker. Mr. Shelley was afterward a pupil of Dudley Buck for several years, and like him settled in Brooklyn as organist of one of the principal churches. In 1887, he became a pupil of Antonin Dvořák, when the Bohemian composer was in this country. It was under the impetus of his personality that Mr. Shelley took up some of his more ambitious compositions. In his song *The Ride*, written especially for this volume, his avowed object was to get away from the tendency to write a lovelorn wail; to write instead a lyric full of dash and rhythm and good cheer. He has succeeded obviously.

REGINALD DE KOVEN (1859)

It sounds very ominous to call so young a man the father of American comic opera, but not when you observe how young a thing is American comic opera. With *Robin Hood*, American comic opera of the better sort may be said to have had its first birthday. Numerous other works by Mr. de Koven have thrown their weight into the cause of refinement, elaborate ensemble and real lyric development.

Mr. de Koven was born at Middletown, Connecticut, April 3, 1859, and spent the years between eleven and twenty-four in Europe, where he studied music under many masters, including Speidel, Lebert and Pruckner at Stuttgart; Huff in Leipzig, and Genée and Von Suppé at Vienna. He also studied singing at Florence under Vannucinni. He therefore entered the field well equipped to accomplish something in American comic opera. But success does not come from teachers alone, and so Mr. de Koven is the victim of much railing on the charge of reminiscence. This is chiefly due to two facts: the first, that it is impossible to write much popular and whistlable music without using the common expressions; and in the second place, because Mr. de Koven has stood in the fierce white light of popularity in which many of his bitterest rivals have failed to arrive, and in which others would have looked perhaps even less original. From hearing and seeing many unproduced American operas, I may the better be able to whisper this scandal: not the only reminiscent operas are those that achieve publicity and success.

Mr. de Koven's work in opera left him little inclination to compose songs, but he has written a few, especially excellent examples of the ballad type, to which he is chiefly inclined. His *Cradle Song* is interesting in its appropriate simplicity, and has an accompaniment of much grace.

RICHARD HENRY WARREN (1859)

Musical dynasties are not common in America, and it is rare that the son succeeds to his father's music. But Mr. Warren, himself a distinguished organist, is a son and pupil of the distinguished organist, George William Warren. He was born in Albany, New York, September 17, 1859, and at the age of twenty-one went to Europe for study and observation, making a second trip abroad in 1886. From 1880 to 1886, he was organist of All Souls Church in New York, and since that time he has been the organist of St. Bartholomew's Church. He was the organizer and conductor of the Church Choral Society, which has made itself noteworthy for producing works never before heard in America. It was for this society that Horatio W. Parker composed his important *Hora Novissima*. Mr. Warren has written much church music, including two complete services. He has also written operettas, a string quartet, and has a distinct knack of instrumentation. He has written very few songs,—which becomes matter for regret when one observes the fascinating simplicity and charm of his *When the Birds go North Again*.

GERRIT SMITH (1859)

One of the best composers in the smaller forms of short songs and short piano pieces is Gerrit Smith, who was born at Hagerstown, Maryland, December 11, 1859. He was graduated at Hobart College in 1876, and went thence to Stuttgart to study music in both its liquid and its frozen form—that is architecture. He came back in a year and studied the organ with Samuel P. Warren, and the piano with Eugene Fair and William Sherwood. After a few years as organist in Buffalo, he went again to Germany and studied the organ with Haupt, and theory with Rohde. Later he placed himself under Merkel and Ritter, and has spent a month with Grieg at the latter's home in Norway. He then became the organist at St. Peter's in Albany, and eventually in New York at the South Church, which is famous for its musical services. He has won much success as a concert organist, having

toured both America and Europe, and has given upward of three hundred free organ recitals at the South Church. He was among the earliest to take up the cause of the American composers, and was one of the founders, and for some years the president, of the Manuscript Society. His compositions, while they include a sacred cantata, *King David*, for voices and orchestra, and many anthems and other church music, are chiefly, to repeat, confined to short songs and short piano pieces. Typically graceful with typical touches of originality is his song *Dreaming*.

WILLIAM ARMS FISHER (1861)

Mr. Fisher was born in San Francisco, California, April 27, 1861, of New England parentage, and studied harmony, organ and piano with John P. Morgan. After a varied business experience, he decided at the age of twenty-nine to take up music professionally, and went to New York, where he studied singing with several teachers, and later with William Shakespeare in London. On returning to New York he became a pupil of Horatio W. Parker in counterpoint and fugue, and of Dvořák in composition and instrumentation. He was instructor in harmony at the National Conservatory for several years, until, in 1895, he went to Boston, where he now lives.

That the song impulse has always been the dominant one in Mr. Fisher's creative work is shown by the fact that more than fifty of his published compositions are in the lyric form. In his very first opus was a striking setting of *Nur wer die Sehnsucht kennt*, since which he has given voice to many and widely varied moods. One has but to mention the lovable group of children's songs, *Posies from a Child's Garden of Verses*, the poetical setting of Shelley's *World's Wanderers*, the rollicking measures of *Falstaff's Song*, the folk-song naïveté of *O for a Breath of the Moorlands*, or the passionate tenderness of *Softly in a Dream*, to show the range of his emotional expression. Mr. Fisher's songs are uniformly well thought from the singer's standpoint, and he has known how to secure his dramatic and lyric effects without violating the canons of good vocal art. He has always contended that a musical composition in order to be ranked as a successful art-product must be adapted to the instrument chosen for its expression — that great ideas must lose part of their greatness if incapable of effective rendition. A song which is representative of his melodic and artistic skill is *When Allah Spoke*, a setting of verses by Arlo Bates, broadly conceived and of wide emotional range.

HENRY HOLDEN HUSS (1862)

Few American composers have a more substantial reputation than Mr. Huss, who combines unusual erudition with dramatic force. He was born in Newark, New Jersey, June 21, 1862. His first teacher was O. B. Boise; in 1883, he went to Munich for three years and studied counterpoint under Rheinberger, winning public mention for efficiency. In 1886, when he was again in America, the Boston Symphony Orchestra produced his *Rhapsody in C Major* for piano and orchestra, the composer playing the piano part, as he has on many similar occasions in the case of this and others of his compositions, notably his very successful piano concerto. Other important compositions of his have been an *Ave Maria* for women's voices, string orchestra, harp and organ; a Polonaise for violin and orchestra, which was brought out in 1889 at the Paris Exposition by Van der Stucken, on the occasion of his concerts of American works; a Violin Concerto, a prelude for orchestra, *To the Night*, and various vocal works with orchestral accompaniment. Among the most notable of these, both for originality and power, are two settings of Shakespeare's texts, *The Death of Cleopatra* and the *Seven Ages of Man*.

The song *My World*, which is presented in this volume, is not built on such elaborate lines as many of his compositions, but it shows his learning in harmony, and the dignity and deep emotion of his musical individuality.

ETHELBERT NEVIN (1862–1901)

Few composers of genuine culture have been content to confine themselves to one form of composition. Men like Chopin, who devote a life to the piano, or like Franz, who expressed himself altogether in songs, are rare. But versatility no more implies importance than quantity implies quality. To both the critical and the lay mind, composers are apt to seem powerful, like Egyptian kings, in direct ratio with the size of the pyramids they may heap together for their monuments. On this account, the work of Ethelbert Nevin is more often judged by its bulk than by its specific gravity. With the exception of a small number of piano lyrics, which reached a considerable popularity and deserved in some cases even more than they received, and with the exception of a pantomime or two and a few song-cycles, his life was entirely given up to the composition of songs. These did not sweep the country as thoroughly as many examples of triumphant music-hall trash, and yet they acquired a popularity enjoyed perhaps by no other American composer, except Stephen C. Foster, who at his best trembled on the razor-edge between the perfect simplicity of folk-song and the maudlin banality of street-song.

Nevin, who was born in Edgeworth, Pennsylvania, November 25, 1862, and died in New Haven, Connecticut, February 17, 1901, may be safely said to be the first American composer who forced his way into the program of song-recitals of the better class; here his songs played a prominent part, both at home and abroad. The encore song was the entering wedge, and it was he who drove it home; latterly the American song has become almost an indispensable feature of any American recital.

The popularity of Nevin's songs and the spontaneity of their lyric flight often deceive the critic as to their dignity. But Nevin was a true songster; he had the lyric fire of a Schubert, whom the public never found hard to understand, once he was presented to them, and whom the student respects for his wonderful compromise between lyric feeling and emotional depth. So Schubert was a revolutionary in the world of song without ever demanding any special training or analysis from his audience. Like Schubert, Nevin has been a distinct influence for the betterment of his native song. He did not form a school, any more than Schubert did, and I cannot pretend that he has the world-wide importance of Schubert, especially as he never ventured into the orchestral field. But we of to-day say of a certain manner that "it suggests Nevin;" and this manner will almost always be found to consist of two qualities: a lyric thrill, more passionate than is characteristic of Anglo-Saxon expression; and an accompaniment which goes its own way, with a passion of its own, a contra-melody of its own, and a marked richness of harmony.

In his children's songs, Nevin has been true to the spirit of childhood, without sacrificing his art. A good proof is found of this in his *Bed-time Song*, included in this volume. Its present form is a revision made shortly before the composer's death; it was originally dedicated to the woman who later became his wife, and to whose artistic support and sympathy he always paid glowing tribute. She has since established a music scholarship in his name for poor children. The song is a fair type of Nevin at his best, with its graceful and gracious and very singable air, the accompaniment full of luscious harmony and subtle modulations into unexpected keys, and the wistful appeal that both comes from and goes to the heart.

FREDERIC FIELD BULLARD (1864–1904)

A field of song which has been chiefly tilled by the cheaper sort of composer, and that without good reason, is what one might call the ballad of bravery. Similarly, the military march, which is supposed to appeal to the noblest and most self-sacrificing emotions, has been chiefly given over to composers who are not only unimportant, but impossible. Perhaps the chief reason why the songs of bravery have been neglected by the more thoughtful composers is, that their psychology is not involved, and their chief virtue is frankness, bordering on bluster. But just this distinction between bravery and bravado is a hard one to keep, and worthy of any composer's attention.

In America, almost the only cultivated musician who gave special attention to this style was Mr. Bullard. He avoided bluster and achieved vigor with pronounced success. He wrote songs not only of soldiers, but also of the roystering brawl of tavern-friends, the breeze and blarney of Irishmen, and the bluff contentment of old salts. In fact, Mr. Bullard's music is distinctly masculine.

This predilection for the non-erotic emotions did not prevent his writing various love songs, ranging from cheerful duets in canon-form to ballads of almost melodramatic force. His graceful lyric *Beam from Yonder Star* is a type of his style in the serenade, and is preferred in a collection such as this to some of his songs more exclusively for bass or baritone singers.

Mr. Bullard was born in Boston, September 21, 1864, and was at first a chemist; but he preferred to devote himself to the qualitative analyses of harmonies of compositions and the molecular energies of melody. At the age of twenty-four, that is, in 1888, he went to Munich as a pupil of Rheinberger. He remained there four years, and after a short sojourn in London and Paris returned to Boston, where he occupied himself with teaching and composing, until his untimely death, June 24, 1904, cut short a career which promised richly a still further achievement.

W. J. BALTZELL (1864)

The editor of *The Étude* shows, as a song-writer, an editorial regard for the meaning of the text. Mr. Baltzell was born December 18, 1864, at Shiremanstown, Pennsylvania. He was educated at Harrisburg, and was graduated at the Lebanon Valley College with first honors. He entered the publishing business for some years, and did not take up music professionally until 1888, when he studied in Boston with Stephen A. Emery (theory) and A. W. Thayer (singing). Later he studied theory in London with Sir J. Frederick Bridge, and singing with W. F. Parker. He also sang in church and trained the boy soloists. In 1891 he returned to America and taught at Reading, Pennsylvania, studying at the same time with Dr. H. A. Clarke at the University of Pennsylvania, for which he received the degree of Mus. Bac. In 1897 he went to Philadelphia and took up editorial work, which was interrupted by a year of teaching the history and theory of music at the Ohio Wesleyan University, Delaware, Ohio.

His compositions have been mainly songs, of which a good example is the rushing emotion of *Thou art Mine*.

HARVEY WORTHINGTON LOOMIS (1865)

Greater New York can add to its contributions to American music Harvey Worthington Loomis, who was born in Brooklyn, February 5, 1865, and has had both his entire musical training and his musical life in New York proper. He is one of the pupils whom Dvořák trained during his sojourn in America. The Bohemian master cannot be credited with giving Mr. Loomis his remarkably distinct and determined musical personality, but he deserves at least the credit for encouraging him to continue along his own lines. Loomis has been left practically alone in America in his special devotion to what may be called pantomimic music in the higher sense of the word. He has not only succeeded in humorous musical expression, but in dramatic and emotional presentation no less, and a number of his pantomimes have been acted with artistic success. On somewhat similar lines are the recitatives, which he calls "musical backgrounds," the music being intended to illuminate and ennoble the recitation of some poem. These musical backgrounds, as his *Sandalphon*, his *Story of the Peartree*, *Story of the Faithful Son* and *The Coming of the Prince*, are in a sense dramatic recitatives of the highest order. The words are to be spoken, not sung indeed, but they are made wonderfully effective by the profound intelligence and the daring imagination with which the piano or the other instrumental parts are written. I know of no other living composer more intensely original with perfect sincerity to the situation, or more fearless in the invention of harmonic novelties which may be compelled by the unhampered progression of the different parts. He seems not to fear any rigor of dissonance, provided it is logically arrived at and not untrue to the spirit of the moment. For this reason many of his piano pieces and accompaniments are difficult to comprehend at the first hearing. But as was the case with Schumann, what looks sometimes to be a small affectation or studied eccentricity, turns out to be the inevitable result of musical candor and directness. This is true of two sorts of compositions in which he excels, laughter-provoking humor and the bitterest tragedy. Loomis has written a great number of songs, and *In the Foggy Dew*, which represents him in this volume, is very characteristic in its rich harmonic scheme, melodic flow and distinct atmosphere.

NATHANIEL IRVING HYATT (1865)

When Mendelssohn founded the " Conservatorium " at Leipzig, he little knew how much it would add to the education of American composers. Among the many who have been taught there is Mr. Hyatt, who was born at Lansingburgh, New York, April 23, 1865, and studied at Troy, New York, with C. A. White and Dr. Jefferey before he went abroad. He was at Leipzig from 1887 to 1892, and his teachers in theory were Schreck and Reinecke, and in piano, Bruno Zwintscher. Returning to America, he taught three years at Troy; then four years at Syracuse University as professor of piano and theory; since which time he has been the head teacher at St. Agnes' School, Albany.

His compositions include a Symphony in A Minor, an overture, *Enoch Arden*, and a string quartet; a suite for two pianos, and various choruses; also various songs, one of the best of which is *The Spring of Love*.

HOMER A. NORRIS (1865)

The French critic Lalo has recently created a great stir by advancing the claim of France to high consideration in Europe as a serious musical entity; he complains that German books ignore French composers, except in the field of light opera, and insists that there are no German symphonists equal to certain of the French. However this may be, it is certain that American music has been too completely under German control, and there is a very welcome relief through the influence of Edward MacDowell, who had some French training, and of Ethelbert Nevin, who lived for some time in Paris and showed much Gallic spirit, and of Norris, who has had all his training in France, and has been an active crusader for the claims of French authority in the theory of music.

Mr. Norris was born in Wayne, Maine, October 4, 1865. He was graduated from the New England Conservatory, and then studied for four years in Paris at the Conservatoire under Théodor Dubois, Guilmant, Gigout and Godard. Returning then to Boston, he occupied himself with teaching and various writings, including two books of harmony and counterpoint on a French basis. He has also composed a concert overture, *Zoroaster*, a cantata, *Nain*, and a number of songs, in almost all of which some distinct and worthy harmonic idea is set forth with unusual sympathy and directness. His song *Dearie* is of the Scotch school, full of candid pathos; underneath its simplicity it shows much musical learning. The ending is full of surprise and yet is enriched with an elegiac regret.

N. CLIFFORD PAGE (1866)

So much of American blood is foreign that it is only natural for an American composer to put the expression of his emotions in various national dialects. Mr. Page was born in San Francisco, California, October 26, 1866, and for many years lived there. His tuition is principally due to one of our most notable composers, Edgar Stillman Kelley, whose influence he shows in many ways, especially in the writing of Chinese music, to which indeed there is much temptation in view of the great number of Chinese in San Francisco. Mr. Page has also shown great interest in Oriental music, as the song *Regrets of Bŏkhära* gives charming proof. He had composed operas at the age of twelve, and claims to have used in later years to advantage some of the ideas that were imbedded in these childish beginnings. At the age of sixteen he began to study music as a career. He became quickly adept in orchestration, and his first opera, composed and orchestrated before he was twenty-one, was produced at San Francisco. Certain of the scenes were laid in Morocco, and the Oriental color is noteworthy. Mr. Page became a conductor at an early age and has done some of his best work in writing incidental music. It was he who wrote the vivid accompaniment to the Chinese dramas, *The Cat and the Cherub* and *Moonlight Blossom*. He has also done other excellent orchestral work, such as a *Caprice*, in which one eight-measure theme is developed through five elaborate movements.

HENRY F. GILBERT (1868)

Of experimenters in novel harmonic effects, we have not many who go so far or reach so striking results as Mr. Gilbert. He was born in Somerville, Massachusetts, September 26, 1868, where he still lives. His first studies were on the violin under Emil Mollenhauer; his teacher in harmony

was George H. Howard, and later, for three years, E. A. MacDowell. He has been interested in Slavic music, and has assisted Professor J. D. Whitney of Harvard University in giving concerts in its illustration.

After six years spent in business without any musical activity, Mr. Gilbert went abroad and heard Charpentier's opera *Louise* in Paris. He was thereby moved to give himself entirely to musical composition. He has written some works for orchestra, and a few songs with orchestral accompaniment; also a piano sonata and various lyrics. His *Croon of the Dew*, reproduced herewith, is an extraordinarily unconventional song, both in subject and in treatment. In view of the thousands of compositions that are poured forth without a new progression or a new combination to their backs, originality of effort is always to be welcomed. When it is evinced with so much emotion and artistic feeling as this composition of Mr. Gilbert's, its reception should be still more cordial.

VICTOR HARRIS (1869)

Another contribution made by New York to the successful musicians of America is Victor Harris, who was born in the metropolis, April 27, 1869, and has won a large fame as the most artistic and successful of accompanists. He is also kept busy as a teacher and coach for operatic singers. In his early years Mr. Harris was well known as a boy soprano. At the age of twenty-six he was assistant-conductor to Anton Seidl. His teacher of harmony was Frederick Schilling.

As would be expected, Mr. Harris, who is so excellent an interpreter of other men's songs, is also

skilful in construction of songs of his own. He has not been especially prolific in them, but those he has written show very graceful melodic contours and are warmly harmonized. A typical song is his *Hills o' Skye*, with its expression of tender melancholy and admirable touches of Scottish color.

HENRY K. HADLEY (1871)

The most welcome qualities that youth can give to art are intense enthusiasm both in joy and grief. There is, however, in the average young creator a fear of his own muscles and his own zeal. In consequence it often happens that one becomes old before he realizes the true charm of youthful exuberance; and we are the victims of this paradox, that most of the young men of talent are trying to write venerably, and most of the old men are aping the manners of the young. When, therefore, we meet a young man who dares to feel and be young, he is thrice welcome. For this reason the music of Mr. Hadley is thrice welcome.

He has written a splendid symphony called *Youth and Life*, and, deserving its title, its sorrow is the wild melancholy of youth, and its joy is the frantic joy of hot blood. Anton Seidl produced this symphony in 1897. Three years later Mr. Hadley brought out a second symphony called *The Seasons*, and a ballet suite was produced by the American Symphony Orchestra. Other orchestral works have met success, and Mr. Hadley has been recently tempted into the field of comic opera.

He was born at Somerville, Massachusetts, December 20, 1871, and was the son of a teacher of music, who furthered his musical education. His teachers in America were Emery, Chadwick, Heindl and Allen, all of Boston. Before he was twenty-one he had written a dramatic overture and other ambitious works. In 1894 he went to Vienna as the pupil of Mandyczevsky, returning to America in 1896. Along with its splendid vigor, Mr. Hadley's music is characterized by a decided harmonic bravery. His music is not self-conscious, and not afraid of itself or the consequences of emotion. In the fervid expression Mrs. Browning gave to her love in the Sonnets which she by a subterfuge of modesty called *Portuguese*, Mr. Hadley has found the inspiration for a very powerful lyric, *How do I Love Thee?* In the sweep of the emotion he has disguised the difficulties of the verse-form, which are somewhat incommensurate with the usual type of lyric, but which here give all the splendor of the words and the sentiments their full value and share in the song.

CHARLES FONTEYN MANNEY (1872)

To adapt the music to the spirit of the words is an ideal which has constantly to be renewed in the world of music, always as a re-discovery. To say that the music should fully express the words is only to say what Peri said in Italy in 1600, and Harry Lawes said in England a few years later, winning thereby Milton's praise; and Gluck said in the next century; and Wagner, Schumann and Franz in the next after that. It is a good thing for composers to keep saying, and it is all the better if they look upon the ancient ideal as their own original discovery, for then they will be the more sincere. An especially good example of musical fidelity to its text is Mr. Manney's *Orpheus with his Lute*. In this poem of Shakespeare's, one of the most charming effects is the very appearance of awkwardness. Just observe the amount of apparent unskilfulness packed into these three lines:

> *Orpheus with his lute made trees*
> *And the mountain-tops that freeze*
> *Bow themselves when he did sing.*

Yet as the song moves on you see that this very effect was intentional, and it is charming. So Mr. Manney in his setting of the poem has begun with the same quaint gaucheries, and develops the same warmth of treatment and charm.

Mr. Manney was born in Brooklyn, New York, February 8, 1872, and as a boy was for several years solo soprano in a vested choir. He began the study of musical theory with William Arms Fisher, and later, after his removal to Boston, he continued his studies with J. Wallace Goodrich and Dr. Percy Goetschius. Besides a number of songs and piano pieces he has published two successful cantatas, as well as a quantity of choral music.

ARTHUR FARWELL (1872)

William Morris was an artist, both in the composing and printing of poetry. We have no American poets who have practised publication as a fine art, but we have a composer who, in addition to writing some of the best American songs, has been impelled to establish a press from which he issues occasional compositions by his fellow-countrymen, in a distinctly artistic manner. This is Arthur Farwell, of the Wa-Wan Press, at Newton Centre, Massachusetts. Born in St. Paul, Minnesota, April 23, 1872, he has made a special study of Indian melodies, and has harmonized many of them and written developments of them. But his own songs do not show any rash effort to express his emotions barbarically; for, after all, we Americans have no more right to ape the musical mannerisms of the strange people whom our forefathers found it so hard to get along with, except at the end of a gun or through the music of wampum, than we have to enslave and call our own the melodies and scales of those unfortunate foreigners whom we imported to this country very much against their will in the steerage of slave-ships. Both the Indian and the so-called Ethiopian schools of music show splendid material for composition, but the European has as much right to these as the American.

Mr. Farwell studied first with Homer A. Norris of Boston, and later in Germany with Humperdinck. This latter teacher seems not to have influenced Mr. Farwell to the same school in which he has himself attained such distinction, for Mr. Farwell's songs are likely to be of a very serious nature and intensely matured sentiment. His song *Wenlock Town* is a remarkably poignant expression of homesickness, and his *Straw Poppy-buds* is notably original. He has set to music four songs by Johanna Ambrosius, that Sappho whose bitterly humble existence did not prevent her poetry from being thrilled with strangely rich refinement of expression and of thought. One of these, *Drücke mich an deine Brust*, or *Meeting*, is reproduced in this volume in its very free but strong translation by Mr. Farwell. The melodic suspensions and anticipations show a certain Wagnerian influence, but they are not imitative and they express the words. The harmonic structure is most unhackneyed, and I find the climax of the song peculiarly haunting.

RUBIN GOLDMARK (1872)

"There are two Goldmarks," exclaimed Dvořák, when the twenty-year-old nephew of the famous Carl Goldmark produced a trio at the Conserva-

tory Concert in New York. The nephew of the eminent German composer was born in New York City, August 15, 1872, and had his first musical training there, going at the age of seventeen to Vienna, where he studied piano with Livonius and Door, and composition with Fuchs. Two years later Mr. Goldmark returned to New York, and became the pupil of Joseffy and Dvořák for a year. In 1892 his health took him to Colorado Springs, where he established a conservatory, and acted as director and lecturer. After spending some years there, he returned to New York, where he now lives.

In 1895 an orchestral theme with variations was produced in New York by Anton Seidl; it had been written by Mr. Goldmark at the age of nineteen. Mr. Goldmark's music is noteworthy for its harmonic originality and experiment; his cantata for orchestra and chorus, *The Pilgrimage to Kevlaar*, being an example of his learning. A piano and violin sonata is another excellent composition. His *Hiawatha Overture* was performed by the Boston Symphony Orchestra, and Mr. Huneker called it "bewilderingly luscious."

In his songs, Mr. Goldmark shows the same vitality and wealth of resource. *The Passionate Shepherd to his Love* is an excellent example of his lyric style.

H. CLOUGH-LEIGHTER (1874)

One of the youngest of American composers, and one of the most artistic in the composition of songs, Mr. H. Clough-Leighter is also to be noted as an exception to the rule that all good American composers go to Germany soon after they are born.

He was born in Washington, District of Co-

lumbia, May 13, 1874, and as a child began his musical studies early under the care of his mother, who taught him harmony as well as piano from the age of five. At nine he was a boy soprano, as was Ethelbert Nevin. His first teacher outside of his home was Dr. E. S. Kimball, under whom he studied theory of music. When his soprano voice left him, he studied composition with Henry Xander. He also spent three years at organ playing and organ construction. At the age of thirteen he entered Columbian University, obtaining a scholarship; but he did not continue his college course. At fifteen he was a professional organist. He also passed the examination in music at Trinity University, Toronto, Canada, under Dr. J. Humphrey Anger. It is small wonder that such close application from so early an age should have broken down his health. At the end of a year of rest, he resumed work.

The thoroughness of his study accounts for the remarkable harmonic richness and freedom of his songs, and his early training as a singer started him on the path of real lyricism. He has well stated his ideal, which has been indeed the ideal of all true song-composers from old Harry Lawes down, though not all of them have so well expressed or so well practised their ideal.

"The objective point with me is to search out and create the most perfect union between the poet's lyrical thoughts and the composer's most sympathetic response to them in his music; the melody of the one being so closely woven and interlaced with the melody of the other, that when once wedded they become inseparable and interdependent. In other words, the memory of one is ever haunted by the memory of the other."

His song *I Drink the Fragrance of the Rose* is

typical of both aspects of his art, the harmonic and the lyric. Swiftly as it rushes on its way, it is yet clothed in all the silks and velvets of rich color.

JOHN PATTON MARSHALL (1877)

A pupil of three of America's best composers,— Mac-Dowell, Chadwick, and Homer Norris, — Mr. Marshall has provided his art with a solid foundation. He was born at Rockport, Massachusetts, January 9, 1877, and came to Boston at sixteen to study the piano and composition with B. J. Lang, later studying also with the composers previously mentioned. He was appointed professor of music at Boston University in 1903, and is also organist and choirmaster at St. John's Episcopal Church in Boston. He has been an enthusiastic student of plainsong, though his compositions are of modern feeling. His publications are of limited number, and include a graceful concert waltz in B flat, and a *Book of Four Songs*, two of them in the old English manner. But of all his songs, his *O Mighty One* is in harmony the richest, and in sentiment the most vital.

DAVID STANLEY SMITH (1877)

In his native city, Toledo, Ohio, where he was born, July 6, 1877, Mr. Smith had lived in a musical atmosphere, his father being an amateur organist, having a pipe organ in the home. He studied at Toledo with S. W. Cushing, A. W. Kortheuer and Mrs. H. B. Jones. During his course at Yale Mr. Smith studied zealously under Horatio Parker, acted as music director and organist at the Centre Church, New Haven, and produced various compositions at other places. On his graduation day, 1900, his *Commencement Ode* was performed under the bâton of Horatio Parker, with a full orchestra, bass solo and chorus of fifty; this being the only time an undergraduate has been granted such an honor. During the same festivities, his *Commencement March* was given by a full orchestra under his own direction. From Yale he went abroad for two years to study under Thuille in Munich, and Widor in Paris. While still abroad he was elected instructor in theory at Yale.

His compositions include various anthems and a number of songs, of which his *Rose Song* has achieved a success its exquisite harmony and sentiment have well earned.

SONGS
BY THIRTY AMERICANS

MATIN SONG

(Original Key)

BAYARD TAYLOR (1825-1878)

JOHN KNOWLES PAINE, Op. 29, N°1

VOICE

PIANO

I let the dear - est dream de-part That

night to love re-vealed, Some ea-ger spir-it in my heart__ My

sleep - ing eyes un-sealed. Yet still 'twas love that led me here And

bids my feet de - lay. A - rise, and light the

dawn, my dear! Look _____ forth, look forth and bring _____ the day.

As out of dark - ness yon-der

star Of whi - test ray is born As birds and blos-soms feel a-

-far ___ The com - ing of the morn, So thou hast dawn'd, and

now art near, To bright - en ___ and to stay: My

be - ing dies in thine, my dear! As ___ day - break dies ___ in

day.

IN THY DREAMS

(Original Key)

Words from the German
by J. S. DWIGHT

DUDLEY BUCK, Op. 67, No 2

*) Original accompaniment for 2 violins, 2 violas and cello.

M L-678-5

6

MI-678-5

keep, And prays for thee ____ while thou'rt a-sleep; Slum-ber sweet

dar - ling dear, slum - ber."

If thro' thy dreams are

ring - ing Sweet ech - oes from the vale, To thee a bird is

sing - ing, sing - ing, 'tis I, _____ 'tis I, _____ the nightin-

gale! Of love and long-ing will I sing, Till dawn to

thee good mor - row bring, _____ Slum - ber sweet, dar - ling dear,

slum - ber! _____

LOOK NOT UPON ME WITH THINE EYES

(Original Key)

W. J. HENDERSON

HOMER N. BARTLETT
Op. 208, №1

ML-679 4

12

TRISTRAM AND ISEULT

(Original Key)

Selected from "Tristram and Iseult"
MATTHEW ARNOLD (1822-1888)

ADOLPH M. FOERSTER
Op.60

Ah, sweet an-gels, let him dream! Keep his eye-lids; let him seem

Not this fe-ver was-ted wight Thinned and paled be-fore his time,

But the bril-liant youth-ful knight___ In the glo-ry
of his prime,___ Sit-ting in the gild-ed barge,___ At thy side, thou
love-ly charge,___ Bend-ing gay-ly
O'er thy hand, I - seult of Ire-land!

up,   And   to Tris - tram   laugh-ing say,_____

"Sir Tris - tram   of thy

cour - te-sy,   Pledge___ me in my   gold - en cup"

Let them   drink   it;   let their

quasi parlando

nay, nay,   thou must not take my hand!   Tris - tram! sweet

love!   we are be - trayed,   out-planned.   Fly,   save thyself,

save_ me!   I dare . not stay."

One last kiss first!_____   "'Tis

KISS ME, SWEETHEART

(Original Key)

JOHN PAYNE

WILSON G. SMITH

ML-681-4

There is no bird in brake or brere, _____ But to his lit-tle mate sings

he. _____ Kiss me, sweet-heart; the spring is here, _____

Con passione e poco slentando

molto espress. *rit.*

And love is lord, is lord of you and me.

a tempo
poco dim. *rall.* *e* *dim.*

Kiss me, sweetheart, the spring is here, Kiss me, sweet-heart, kiss me, sweet-

a tempo *colla voce*

Con passione e poco slentando

molto espress.

dear. _____ Kiss me, sweetheart, the spring is here. _____

Kiss me, sweetheart; the spring is here, _____ And love is lord, is lord of

rit. *poco dim.*

you and me. Kiss me, sweetheart; the spring is here, Kiss me, sweet-

rall. *e* *dim.*

heart; kiss me, ___ sweetheart.

colla voce *pp* *pp* *dim. e rit.* *pp*

APRIL WEATHER

(Original Key)

EDNAH PROCTOR CLARKE

JAMES H. ROGERS

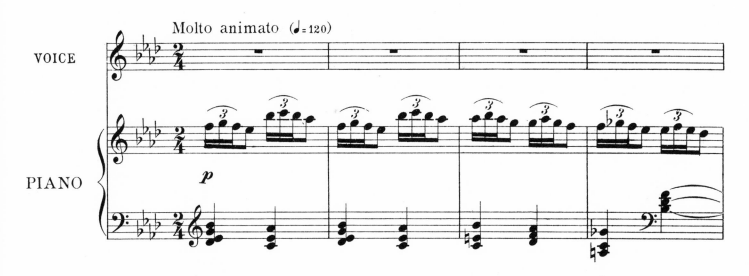

Be - loved, it was A-pril weather,____ When Love went

down ____ the wild - ing way, The

4-39-61445-5

lit - tle birds on bloom - y spray Were

poco a poco cresc.

cock - ing head and preen - ing feath-er. Be -

cresc.

molto cresc. *poco allargando* *ƒ*

lov - ed, it was A - pril weath - - er, When

L.H.

molto cresc.

a tempo

Love went down the wild - ing way.

L.H.

To E. A. Huber

A NORTHERN ROMANCE

(Original Key, Eb minor)

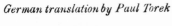

ANDREW LANG (1844 -)
German translation by Paul Torek

HENRY B. PASMORE

My love dwelt__ in a north-ern__ land A
Mein Lieb - ster__ wohnt' in fern - em__ Land, ein

tow - er dim in a for - est green Was his,_____
Schloss, von grü - nem__ Wald be - grenzt, war sein,

Copyright MDCCCXC by Oliver Ditson Co.

ML-682- 5

And__ far a - way the__ sand,_____ And gray
und__ weit der Dü - nen__ sand und wei - sser

wash of the waves was__ seen, The wo - ven for - est__
Wel - len - schaum er - glänzt'_____ durch dicht_____ ver -

boughs,__ the__ boughs be - tween._____
web - tes__ Wald - ge - zweig._____

thro' the northern summer night The sunset slowly
in des Nordlands Dämmerschein die Sonne langsam

died away, And herds of strange deer, silver white, Came
starb dahin, und selt'ne Hirsche, silberreins, er-

And
Und

gleam - ing thro' the___ for - est gray, And fled___ like___

glänz - ten durch den___ Wald so grün, und floh'n___ wie___

ghosts___ be - fore the day.___

Gei - ster___ vor dem Tag.___

I know not if the for - est green Still gir - dles round that

Ich weiss nicht ob das Wal - des-grün noch jetzt das grau - e

cas - tle gray, I know not if, the boughs be - tween, The

Schloss um - ragt, nicht, ob die wei - ssen Hir - sche flieh'n durch

IF LOVE WERE NOT

(Original Key)

FLORENCE EARLE COATES

CLAYTON JOHNS

ML-683-3

bird would build, if love were not, No   flow'r com-pla-cent bloom;   The

sun-set clouds would   lose ____ their   dyes, ____   The

light would fade from beau - ty's   eyes; ____   The

THE RIDE

(Original Key, D)

ANNA ALICE CHAPIN

HARRY ROWE SHELLEY

ML-684-11

glimpse, then are past, are ___ past. The riv - er

gleams ___ blue as we fol - low it fast

The scent of the pines to the wind ___ gives zest,

As it roars ___ in our face on the cold hill's crest; ___ The

wind grows wild and the weath-er is gray;— The clouds are

low all o - ver the sky,——— and the plains re -

sound ——— to the wild bird's cry,——— And fierce strange

voi - ces all join——— to say——— "Ho! gal -

lop, and gal - lop and gal - - lop,

rit. - - - - *a tempo*

gal - - lop — a way _____

colla voce

a tempo

f

Come

down in your sad - dle and sit __ to the leap! __ The

rug - ged moors like an o - cean sweep, The hed-ges and rocks rise high be-fore,

And a-far___ roams the sea on its lone - ly shore:___

And a - round us the pale mists i - ci - ly creep,___ Quick!

down in___ your sad - dle,___ and up to the leap!___ Now

gal - lop, and gal - lop and gal - lop a - way!

To think___ or con - sid - er we may not stay,

The jumps are hard and the way___ is rough,

But the joy___ of the race (and is that not e - nough?)___ Is

on ___ us, is on us is on ___ us to - day, ___ Look!

see, ___ through the trees, the sea ___ far a - way ___

Gal - lop a - way to the yearn - ing sea! ___ O - ho! how it laughs, o - ho, how it laughs,

48

CRADLE SONG

(Original Key)

THOMAS BAILEY ALDRICH (1836-)

REGINALD DE KOVEN

ML-685-3

WHEN THE BIRDS GO NORTH AGAIN

(Original Key, C minor)

ELLA HIGGINSON   RICHARD HENRY WARREN

ML-686-2

53

ML-686-2

To Miss Jeanne Faure

DREAMING

(Original Key)

GERRIT SMITH

GERRIT SMITH

The day when first I met thee, 'Twas in some Spir - it - land, My soul will ne'er for - get thee, Though fate with-hold thine

ML-687-2

WHEN ALLAH SPOKE

(Original Key, B)

ARLO BATES (1852 -   )

WILLIAM ARMS FISHER
Op.14, №1

In moderate time without dragging (♩ = about 63)

VOICE

PIANO

mf

con pedale

Was I not thine when Al - lah spoke the

word Which formed from smoke the sky? Were not our

fz   *mf*

dim.

twin hearts one ___ when heav - en heard the stars, the

p

Copyright MCMII by Oliver Ditson Company
International Copyright Secured

ML-688-6

With breadth (♩ = about 84)

Canst thou then doubt that while ____ the a-ges roll ____

Our be-ing one shall be? _____

As flame and light are one, so is my soul

One, O my love, with thee, As flame and light are

one _____ so is my soul with thee,

One with thee, One with thee.

The ebb - ing

star floods of the Judg - ment day shall leave my

60

ML-688-6

MY WORLD

(Original Key, A♭)

KATRINA TRASK

HENRY HOLDEN HUSS

ML-689 - 2

world, a world!

Lo! in the depths of thine eyes, Glis - tens a 'neb - u - lous light,— I

fol - low it day and night, And find, to my soul's sur - prise, My

world!_____ My world!_____

*) Be exact in the duration of this tone, no ritardando

ML - 689-2

To Miss Anne Paul

A BED-TIME SONG.

(Original Key, F)

LILLIAN DYNEVOR RICE

ETHELBERT NEVIN

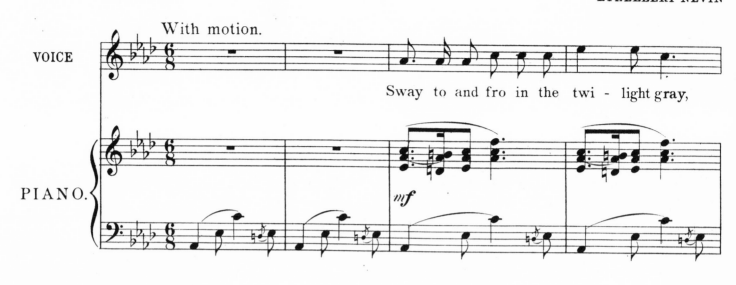

Sway to and fro in the twi - light gray,

This is the fer-ry for Shad-ow-town; It al - ways sails at the end of day,

Just as the dark-ness is clos-ing down. Rest, lit-tle head, on my shoul - der, so; A

Orchestra parts, complete, may be obtained of the publishers, price 50¢

4-47-61785-3

To Mr. Stephen Townsend

BEAM FROM YONDER STAR
A SERENADE

(Original Key, G)

WILLIAM PRESCOTT FOSTER

FREDERIC FIELD BULLARD

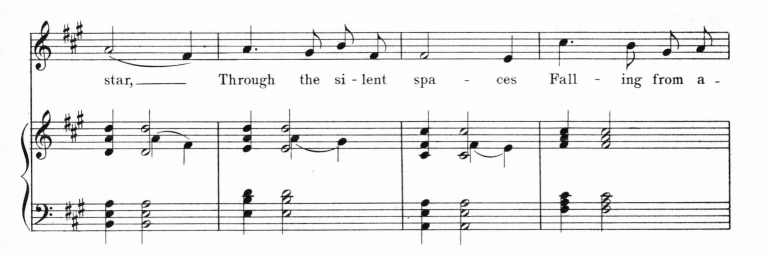

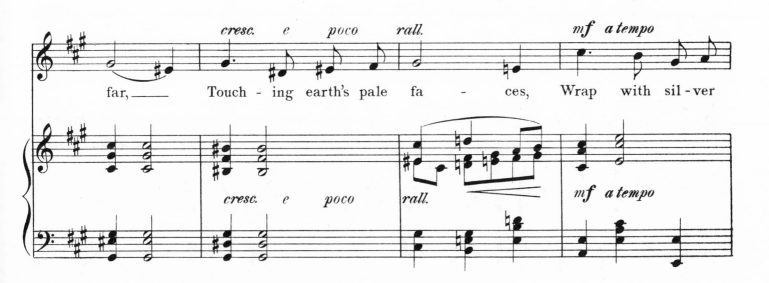

Copyright MDCCCXCVI by Fred. Field Bullard

ML.-690-3

light _____ Her, who soft - ly sleep - ing lies be - neath thy

sight, be-neath thy sight, _____ I her vig - il__ keep -

ing. Gen - tly, gen - tly

rest _____ On her eye-lids ten - der. Touch her brow and

THOU ART MINE

(Original Key)

EDMUND CLARENCE STEDMAN (1833-)

W. J. BALTZELL

Words used by permission of the author

ML-691-7

arms thou art cling - ing; For my ___ ear a - lone ___ thou ___ art sing - ing A

song, ___ a song, ___ a song ___ which no stran-ger hath

heard. ___ But a - far from me yet, like a bird, ___ Thy

soul in some re - gions un - stirr'd ___ On its mys - tic-al cir - cuit is

wing - ing On its mys - tic-al cir - cuit is wing - ing, Thou art

mine,_____ thou art mine,_____ thou art mine._____

Thou art mine, thou art mine, I have made thee mine own;__

Hence-forth we are min-gled to-geth - er. But in

spir - it Is as far____ from my grasp,____ is as free,____

As the stars____ from the moun-tain tops____

be,____ As the pearl in the depths____ of the

sea From the por - tion-less king that would wear it. Thou art

IN THE FOGGY DEW

(Original Key)

HARVEY WORTHINGTON LOOMIS

4-82-63535-5

78

long - ing sore for Ire - land in the fog - gy dew.

The sun he shines all day here, so fierce and fine, With

ne'er a wisp of mist at all to dim his shine; The

sun, he shines all day here from skies of blue, But he

4-82-63535-5

hides his face in Ire - land in the fog - gy dew.

The maids go out to milk - ing in the pas - tures gray;

The sky is green and gold - en at the dawn of day,

And

(on the long low)

in the deep-drenched mead-ows the hay___ lies___ new, And the

espress.

corn is turn-ing yel-low in the fog-gy dew._____

Ma -

molto espress. e più lento

vrone! if I might feel___ now the dew up-on my face, And the

mf   legato

To my wife

THE SPRING OF LOVE

(Original Key)

STOPFORD A. BROOKE (1832-)

NATHANIEL IRVING HYATT

A lit-tle sun,___ a lit-tle rain,___ A

ML-692-4

soft wind blowing from the west, _____ And woods _____ and fields are

sweet a-gain And warmth _____ with-in the mountain's breast, And

warmth _____ with - in _____ the moun - tain's

breast.

A lit-tle love, ___ a lit-tle

trust, ___ A soft im-pulse, ___ a sud-den

dream, ___ And life, ___ as dry as

des - ert dust, Is fresh - er than a

Più animato
moun - tain stream, Is fresh-er than a moun - tain
rit.
p Più animato
cresc.
stream, Is fresh - er than a moun - tain
stream, a moun - - tain,
f
moun - tain stream.
f
ffz

To Mr. George Dwight

DEARIE

(Original Key)

HERBERT RANDALL

HOMER A. NORRIS

4-69-62844-3

87

ro - sy, dear, The heath-er a' sae sweet,— The but-ter-flies sae

yel - low then, When you played at my feet. But

noo the days are a' sae dark! Syne ye hae gaen sae far, Ah!

well! my dear-ie, life's too lang, Syne ye hae gaen a-

4-69-62844-3

THE REGRETS OF BŎKHÄRA

"It is related of Roduki, that the prince under whom he lived, having removed his court from Bŏkhärä to Herât, became so attached to the latter city that he delayed his return, much to the regret of
his courtiers, who employed the powers of the poet to induce the monarch to give up his new passion
and restore them to their homes and friends.   Roduki fully entered into their views, and the follow-
ing verses, sung with great feeling to the *barbut* or viol, on which instrument he was a skillful per-
former, accomplished the end desired, and the prince, Umir Nussar, again took route to Bŏkhärä."

(Original Key, D minor)

From the Persian of Roduki

N. CLIFFORD PAGE

ML-693-5

ff *Buoyantly:– with increasing animation*

hail! Bŏk – hä – ra, land of flow – ers!

Our___ prince moves proud – ly on;___ He

goes___ to glad thy sun – ny bowers,___ He

asks___ thy___ smile a – lone. The

wav - ing cy - press seeks his na - tive groves, The

ris - ing moon the fir - ma - ment it loves. Ah!

CROON OF THE DEW

(Original Key)

GEORGE TURNER PHELPS

HENRY F. GILBERT

Words used by permission of the author

*)There should be no interruption in the flow of the music from ✗ to ✗

sky,_____ Melts be-yond reach_ of eye,_____

Cool - eth the af - ter - noon_____ To_ em - er-ald eve-ning swoon.____

Soft is the bed of moss,____ Moon - light faint - ly a - cross.____

To G.C, in affection

THE HILLS O' SKYE

(Original Key)

WILLIAM McLENNAN

VICTOR HARRIS
Op. 23, No 1

Note. The English equivalent of the Scotch may be freely used.

ML-695-6

storm-beat hills o' Skye._____ Ah!_____

I hae wan-dered miles fu' man-y,_____ I hae mark'd fu' man-y a change, I hae won me gear in plen-ty,_____ In this land sae fair, but

by_____ But it turns hame to Dun - ve - gan, By the

storm beat hills o' Skye. Oh, my heart!____ My

wear-y wear-y heart! By the storm-beat hills o' Skye_____ Ah!

To Mrs. Katherine Bloodgood

HOW DO I LOVE THEE?

(SONNET FROM THE PORTUGUESE, № XLIII)

ELIZABETH BARRETT BROWNING (1806-1861)   *(Original Key)*   HENRY K. HADLEY
Op. 20, № 3

ML-696-6

need,   by sun   and

can - - dle - light. _____   I

love   thee   free - ly,   as   men   strive   for

Right;   I   love   thee   pure - ly   as

men turn from Praise. I love _____ thee____

with the passion put to use In my old

griefs, and with my child-hood's faith _____ I

love ____ thee with a love _____ I

seemed to lose with my lost saints

I love thee with the breath,

Smiles, tears of all my life!

and if God choose, I shall but

ORPHEUS WITH HIS LUTE

SONG from "HENRY THE EIGHTH"

(Original Key, D♭)

WILLIAM SHAKESPEARE (1564-1616)　　　　　CHARLES FONTEYN MANNEY, Op. 3, Nº 5

ML-697-3

There had made a last-ing spring, There had made a last-ing
spring.
Ev-'ry thing that heard him play, E'en the bil - lows
of the sea, Hung their heads and then lay by, _____

Hung their heads and then lay by. In sweet mu - sic is such

art, _____ Kill - ing care and grief of heart _____

f broadly   *rit. e dim.*
Fall a-sleep, or hear-ing, die,   Fall a-sleep, or hear-ing, die.

MEETING

(DRÜCKE MICH AN DEINE BRUST)

JOHANNA AMBROSIUS
Translated by A. F.

(Original Key)

ARTHUR FARWELL

4-79-63879-3

lips to mine___ Give, O give for ev - er,
durst - 'gen Mund___ Lan - ge, ach, nur lan - ge'!

Fear nor fate nor death shall hold Pow'r that kiss to
Nichts gleicht auf den Er - den - rund Die - sem heil - 'gen

sev - er. Deep with - in my thirst - ing soul___
Klan - ge. Sen - ke dei - nen Son - nen - blick___

THE PASSIONATE SHEPHERD TO HIS LOVE

(Original Key)

CHRISTOPHER MARLOWE (1564-1593)

RUBIN GOLDMARK

M L-698-9

dale and field, And all the crag - gy moun - tains yield.

There we shall sit up - on the rocks, And watch the shep - herds

feed their flocks. By shal - low riv - ers, to whose falls Me -

lo - dious birds sing mad - ri - gals.

There will I make thee beds of ros - es,

And a thou - sand fra - grant po - sies, A

cap of flow - ers and a kir - tle, Em - broi - dered all with

leaves of myr - tle, A gown made of the

i - vy buds, With cor - al clasps and

am - ber studs. And if _____ these

p cresc. sempre - - -

pleas - ures may _____ thee move _____ Come

live with me, and be _____ my love, Come

ff

f

live with me and be_____ my love, and

be____ my love, my love._____

rit. a tempo

rit. f a tempo

dim.

Thy

mp

sil - ver dish - es for thy meat, As pre - cious as the

p grazioso

thy de - light each May morn - ing, _____

If these de - lights thy mind may move,

If these de - lights thy mind may

move, _____ Then live with me and

be__ my love, Then live with me and be__ my love, Then live with me and be__ my love, and be__ my love, and be__ my love, my love.

To my dear Mother

I DRINK THE FRAGRANCE OF THE ROSE

(Original Key)

CHARLES HANSON TOWNE

H. CLOUGH-LEIGHTER
Op. 19, No 1

ML-699-5

The rose is for - ev - er __

giv - ing, Giv - ing, for - ev - er __ giv - - -

ing.

Tempo I.

To Miss Anna Miller Wood

O MIGHTY ONE
(O MAÎTRE DE TOUT)
SONG from "IZEYL"

(Original Key, E♭)

ARMAND SILVESTRE (1839-1901)
Translated by Charles Fonteyn Manney

JOHN P. MARSHALL

ML-700-4

might - y ce - dar.
cê - dre gé - ant.
Thou, who in wrath art arm'd with the
Toi, dont la fou - - dre est la com -

thun - der,
pa - gne,
On me a - lone let ven - geance
Tu peux sur moi ven - ger les

fall.
Dieux.
Strong is the ce - dar,
Je suis le cê - dre
strong am I,
dé - ja vieux,

Strike a - lone the tree on the moun - tain.
Frap - pe l'ar - bre sur la mon - ta - gne.

ML-700- 4

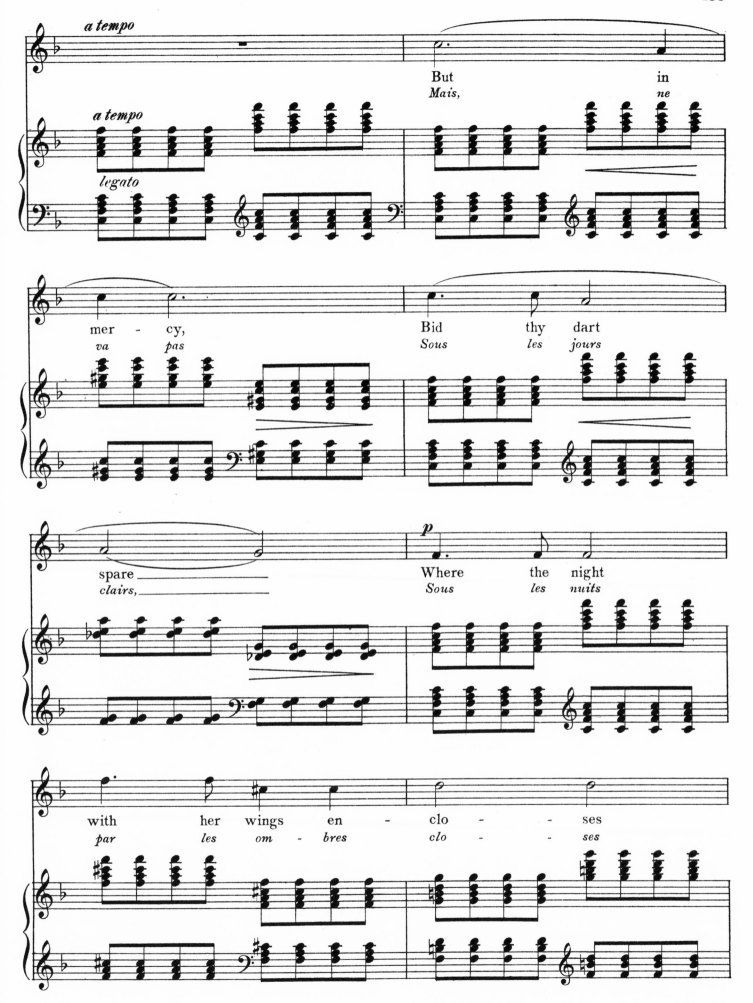

134

Fond - - ly the spring - - time, the
Fau - - cher la jeu - nes - - se, la jeu -

spring - - time of ro - - ses, And where the
nes - - se of des . ro - - ses, A - vec le

sun - - bright day_____ is
tran - - chant des_____ é -

fair._____
clairs._____

ML-700-4

To Miss A.H.H.

ROSE SONG

(Original Key, Db)

CHARLOTTE FISKE BATES
(Mme Adolphe Rogé)

DAVID STANLEY SMITH

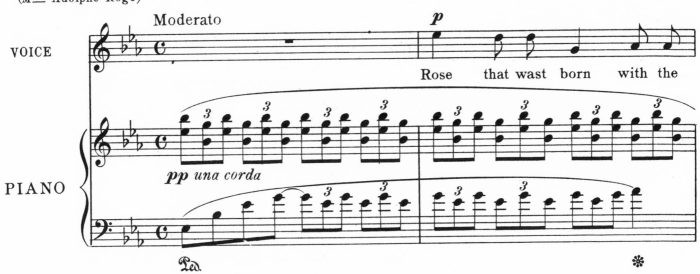

Rose that wast born with the

morn - ing   And hast lived   and died   for

me,   Here   in the dusk   of the

ML-701-3

136